The Ghost House Guide to Ghosts

*A Definitive Catalogue of Ghosts, Ghost Butts, Ghost Horses,
Phantoms, Specters, and Other Weird Ghost Things*

Ghost Writer
JASON STEELE

For the ghost in all of us.

The Real Author
(Identity withheld for ghost reasons.)

Introduction

Ghosts are everywhere, if you really think about it. Even when you can't see them they are lurking, waiting to put their gross ghost butts all over your face. It's unsanitary. We shouldn't have to deal with so many creepy ghosts, but that is the price of living on a ghost planet.

The most we can do in a situation this spooky and shameful is learn about our ghostly tormentors - who they are and what they want. That is what this book is for. It is a catalogue of every type of ghost. Knowledge is power, and ghost knowledge is ghost power.

Even though this book contains a list of every type of ghost, do not assume it is all there is to know about them. Ghosts are weird and surprising. The moment you think you finally understand a ghost it will start dripping goo everywhere or something weird like that.

If you see a ghost that does not match any ghost listed in this book, do not be fooled. The ghost is simply trying to trick you. If you observe the nature of their trick you might be able to determine what type of ghost it is. Memorizing all of the different types of ghosts may help you see through these tricks much quicker.

I do not remember the first time I saw a ghost. I have seen so many, and they have started to blur together in my brain. I call this "ghost blur" and it is the first sign that you have seen too many ghosts and could really use a break. I cannot take a break. I recommend that you take breaks.

Do not share this book with your friends or even your family. One day they might be ghosts themselves - do you want them to know that you are on to their spooky tricks? You can never get the upper hand with a ghost, but sometimes you can get the lower hand. Most ghosts don't even have hands. They just have weird cold tendrils. Tendrils are gross.

I believe that ghosts might control certain factions within the various governments of the world. I know this is a lot for you to take in but I am certain that it is true. After learning about all of the different types of ghosts you will understand what I mean. I do not think they have an agenda. They are ghosts, they just do things.

If a ghost sees you reading this book, do not worry. Lots of people read lots of books. Ghosts are always watching but they are also pretty stupid. Some ghosts are super smart but even the smart ones are pretty dumb. I'm just saying don't freak out if a ghost sees you reading this book because it probably won't understand the significance.

If you yourself one day become a ghost please leave me alone. There are too many ghosts already bothering me and to be honest it is getting super frustrating. It's hard to take a shower when there are twenty or so ghosts just floating there for no reason.

I hope that you find this guide useful, and that it opens your eyes to the terror world of ghosts. Take care of yourself. You can do anything. We are all in this together. Life has no meaning.

"If you fight with ghosts you should be careful lest ye thereby become a ghost. And if thou gaze long into an abyss, the ghosts hanging out in there will also gaze into thee."

- *Nietzsche, Famous Ghost Expert*

GHOST TYPE
"Regular Ghost"

LOCATION
Spooky houses, weird streets.

DISTINCTIVE CHARACTERISTICS
Is a ghost.

SMELLS LIKE
Mildew.

DESCRIPTION
These are by far the most common type of ghosts. They are usually seen floating around old houses or just sort of standing next to broken street lights. You can tell they are a ghost and not a person pretending to be a ghost because they have (like all ghosts) inhumanly sexy butts. There are too many ghosts and I wish they would just go away.

DANGEROUS?
Not very, although they will often try to put their perfect ghost butts right on your face, which could cause a psychological or spiritual crisis.

WHAT TO DO IF YOU SEE ONE
For every regular ghost you see there are a hundred or so you do not see. I don't think you can avoid these. There is probably one putting its butt on your face right now. I'm sorry, I wish there was more I could do.

GHOST TYPE
"Angry Ghost"

LOCATION
Murder sites, old ships.

DISTINCTIVE CHARACTERISTICS
Grumpy ghost face.

SMELLS LIKE
Warm birds.

DESCRIPTION
An angry ghost is usually angry because it was murdered or betrayed or something. Or maybe it died in a stupid way like falling out of a hot air balloon and it doesn't know how to deal with that. If you see a ghost with an angry face it's probably an angry ghost, unless it's a regular ghost trying to trick you.

DANGEROUS?
Yes, angry ghosts are very dangerous. You should avoid these because they will try and shove you or bonk your head like you're some sort of simpleton. They have been known to throw things for no reason.

WHAT TO DO IF YOU SEE ONE
Whatever you do, don't tell an angry ghost to calm down because that will just make it even more angry. I don't really know what to do with these ghosts besides just sort of wait it out and hope they vanish into smoke.

GHOST TYPE
"Sad Ghost"

LOCATION
Graveyards, rainy nights, your own house sometimes.

DISTINCTIVE CHARACTERISTICS
Very sad face and eyes.

SMELLS LIKE
Old blankets.

DESCRIPTION
A sad ghost is a ghost that is all depressed about being a ghost or something. I don't mind these ghosts that much because I get sad too, but I wish they weren't so loud. Some of us have a hard time sleeping and sad ghosts just make it worse. I wish I could make them less sad but I can't do that with anybody.

DANGEROUS?
Not really, unless you really don't like moaning.

WHAT TO DO IF YOU SEE ONE
Nothing seems to make them happy, not even ice cream. But everyone gets sad sometimes so give them a break, and maybe try to give them a hug even though you can't because they are a ghost.

GHOST TYPE
"Moaning Ghost"

LOCATION
Outside at night.

DISTINCTIVE CHARACTERISTICS
Moans for no reason.

SMELLS LIKE
Sweaty animals.

DESCRIPTION
These ghosts are like the sad ghosts, but they aren't sad and so I'm not sure why they're moaning. But that's pretty much all they do. If you try to have a conversation with a moaning ghost it won't go anywhere because all they do is moan. I don't have a lot of respect for these ghosts because if you're going to do something you should have a reason.

DANGEROUS?
I don't know, probably not. They're annoying though and annoyance is a kind of danger.

WHAT TO DO IF YOU SEE ONE
Don't even try to reason with it or get it to stop moaning because it won't work. If you like to moan then I'm sure these ghosts are great and you'll have a lot in common, otherwise I would avoid them.

GHOST TYPE
"Cool Ghost"

LOCATION
Skate parks, arcades, behind the bleachers at schools.

DISTINCTIVE CHARACTERISTICS
Wears sunglasses and usually carries a skateboard.

SMELLS LIKE
Cigarettes.

DESCRIPTION
I don't think these ghosts are that cool but what do I know. Most of them carry skateboards but I've never even seen them skate. I don't like to throw the word poser around all willy-nilly but sometimes I think it might be true. I wish they didn't wear sunglasses because I like to be able to see a ghost's eyes. It freaks me out when I can't tell if they're looking at me or not.

DANGEROUS?
No, although I smell cigarettes when they are around and I'm worried about second hand smoke. I will update this book if I end up with cancer.

WHAT TO DO IF YOU SEE ONE
No matter how hard you try they don't seem to think you're cool or want to hang out with you. You don't need their approval even if you really want it. Maybe they'll let you use their skateboard. I doubt it though.

GHOST TYPE
"Phantom"

LOCATION
Churches, cathedrals, opera houses.

DISTINCTIVE CHARACTERISTICS
Wears stylish clothes, which is weird for a ghost.

SMELLS LIKE
Roses and gunpowder.

DESCRIPTION
Phantoms are ghosts that have gotten dressed up and are trying to act all smart. Sometimes they seem way smarter than you, but I think that's a ghost trick. Phantoms always have some sort of plan, but their plans are really dumb when you think about it for more than a minute.

DANGEROUS?
Yes, their plans might involve dropping things on you or setting stuff on fire. Don't make enemies with a phantom because it's really not worth all the trouble.

WHAT TO DO IF YOU SEE ONE
Just sort of nod and be on your way. You do not want a phantom in your life. Trust me. I had a phantom in my life named Jet and it was cool for a while but things didn't really work out. I know that you need to make your own decisions but it would feel wrong not to warn you, given what I know.

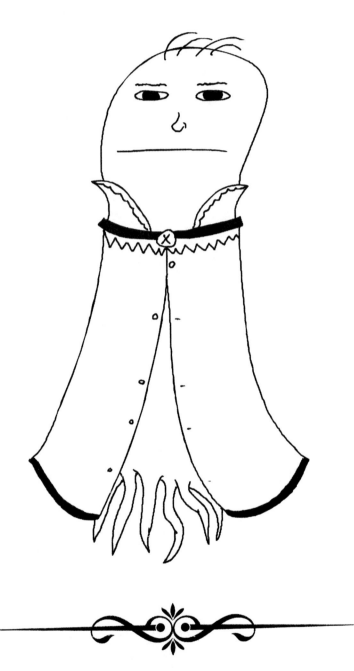

GHOST TYPE
"Screaming Eye"

LOCATION
Catacombs, ancient tombs, dark basements.

DISTINCTIVE CHARACTERISTICS
Is a huge screaming eye ball.

SMELLS LIKE
Sticky floor stuff.

DESCRIPTION
There isn't a whole lot to say about these. They are huge screaming eyes and that's pretty weird. I don't know how these ghosts came to be and to be honest I don't really care. I don't think screaming eyes should exist but then again I don't really like most ghosts. I've never had one touch me which is a miracle.

DANGEROUS?
I'm not sure, they seem super dangerous but I've never seen one do anything besides scream a lot and look unnatural.

WHAT TO DO IF YOU SEE ONE
You can let it look at you for a bit if you don't want to be rude, but do not let it get eye juice on you. Their eye juice is sticky and gross. A good pair of earplugs would help with all the screaming and commotion.

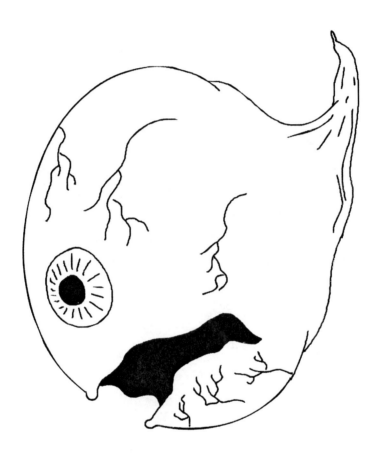

GHOST TYPE
"Specter"

LOCATION
Houses, forests, creepy shops.

DISTINCTIVE CHARACTERISTICS
Hiding just out of sight.

SMELLS LIKE
Not sure.

DESCRIPTION
A specter is a ghost that you can't really see that well because it's hiding behind a wall or a tree or something. I don't know if they're shy or being creeps. Sometimes I see one watching when I'm taking a shower. But they also watch when I'm just sitting there not doing anything. I don't care that they look but I wish I knew why.

DANGEROUS?
I don't think so. They could be planning something but if they are it's taking a really long time.

WHAT TO DO IF YOU SEE ONE
There isn't much you can do about these, if you approach one it will fade away which is really frustrating. I leave them little notes sometimes but I'm not sure if they get them. I hope they do. I put a lot of thought into my notes. A good note can really brighten your day.

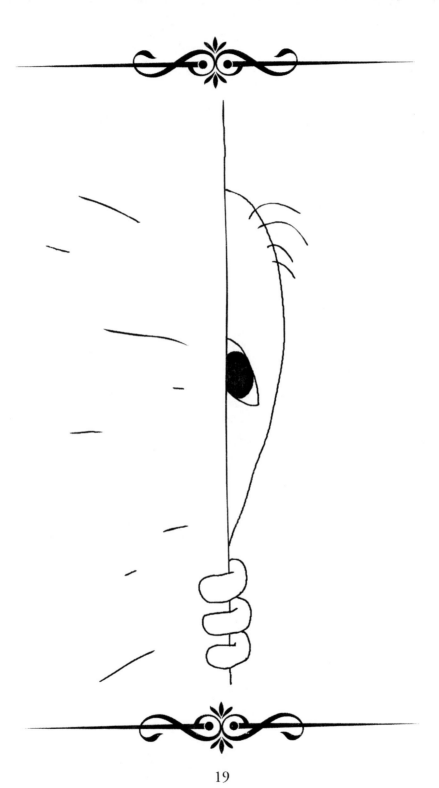

GHOST TYPE
"Wraith"

LOCATION
Foggy hills, dusty battlefields, forgotten roads.

DISTINCTIVE CHARACTERISTICS
Super scary looking.

SMELLS LIKE
Rotting wood.

DESCRIPTION
Wraiths are one of the scariest types of ghosts. They have this "no good" look about them that makes you want to run away. I don't see them very often but when I do it's a bad experience. They howl a lot in a really alarming pitch and are much faster than regular ghosts. I once saw a wraith drain the life out of a chipmunk and it was one of the most upsetting things I've seen in my life.

DANGEROUS?
Very dangerous, these things are the worst. I wouldn't be surprised if they all turned out to be murderers and thieves.

WHAT TO DO IF YOU SEE ONE
Run away. Don't bother trying to get your car to start because it probably won't. Find a supermarket or something because I don't think a wraith will follow you in there. I've never seen a wraith in a supermarket.

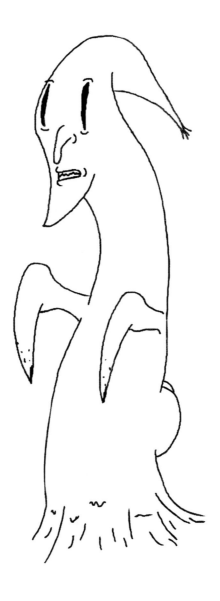

GHOST TYPE
"Beth"

LOCATION
Ghost houses.

DISTINCTIVE CHARACTERISTICS
The only ghost I ever loved.

SMELLS LIKE
Peaches and wet cement.

DESCRIPTION
The moment I met Beth I knew she was different than other ghosts. I usually don't like ghosts all that much but Beth was pretty great. I don't know how things went so wrong but we don't really talk anymore. I wish things could have worked out between us but life just doesn't go your way sometimes. Every so often I think I see Beth looking at me from across the room but it always ends up being just a regular ghost.

DANGEROUS?
Only if you never expected to fall in love.

WHAT TO DO IF YOU SEE ONE
It's worth it even if your heart gets broken forever. I hope that you find a Beth of your own and that things turn out nice.

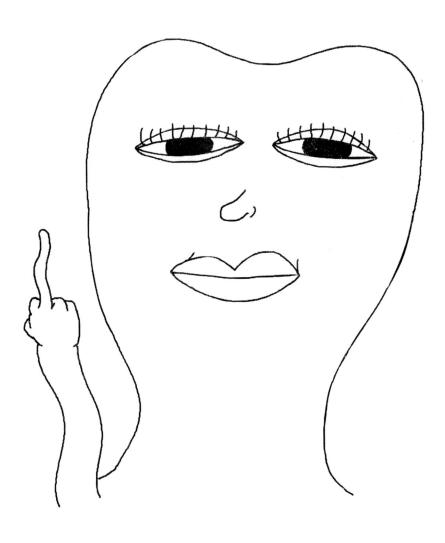

GHOST TYPE
"Ghost Horse"

LOCATION
Everywhere, which is weird.

DISTINCTIVE CHARACTERISTICS
Is a horse and a ghost.

SMELLS LIKE
What you would expect a dead horse to smell like.

DESCRIPTION
I don't know why there are so many ghost horses around and not all that many ghosts of other animals. Ghost horses like to play a lot of jokes and sometimes it's all in good fun but other times they take it too far. I tried to make some ghost horse friends, I really did, but it just didn't work out. They don't seem to care about anything except jokes and tricks.

DANGEROUS?
Sometimes they play dangerous tricks and people could get hurt. We're not all ghosts and they don't seem to understand that.

WHAT TO DO IF YOU SEE ONE
Don't shake their hooves or walk with them through any doors because you're just going to get sticky stuff on your hands and a bucket of ghost goo on your head. I think they like apples, but then again so do most ghosts.

GHOST TYPE
"Buttly Soul"

LOCATION
Wherever you're just trying to eat and want to be left alone.

DISTINCTIVE CHARACTERISTICS
Is a flying butt.

SMELLS LIKE
Cinnamon for some reason.

DESCRIPTION
These might just be ghost tricks, I don't know. They're just a butt with wings and a halo and that's really stupid. I see them flying around sometimes and I don't want to be a ghost racist and say they don't exist but I do wonder. They don't do any gross butt stuff which is a relief but they only seem to show up when I'm trying to eat and I don't know why.

DANGEROUS?
No, they just sort of float around.

WHAT TO DO IF YOU SEE ONE
They only float around for a couple minutes so you can usually wait it out with these. They do get right up in your face which is the worst but I'm not sure what you can do about that. I suppose they could provide an interesting photo opportunity for your ghost scrapbook.

GHOST TYPE
"Owls"

LOCATION
Forests, outside windows.

DISTINCTIVE CHARACTERISTICS
They look like regular owls.

SMELLS LIKE
A bird.

DESCRIPTION
I'm pretty sure some owls are just ghosts that look like owls. I don't think they are dead owl spirits, I think they're ghosts who decided to live as owls. Sometimes I'll see an owl looking at me and I recognize the look as a "ghost glance." I don't understand why ghosts would want to be owls but it's not my place to judge especially when they're not bothering me.

DANGEROUS?
No, they don't even really pay attention to you.

WHAT TO DO IF YOU SEE ONE
Maybe give it some bird seeds, or whatever owls eat. If it is an owl it will appreciate the food, and if it is a ghost it will probably appreciate the thought. It's nice to know that someone is thinking about you.

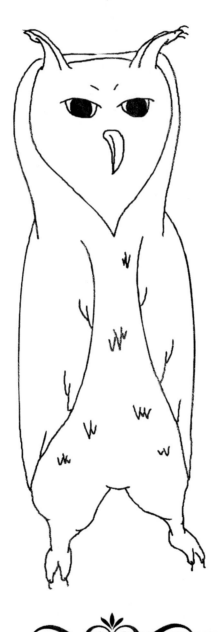

GHOST TYPE
"Goo Ghost"

LOCATION
Floating around furniture and other things that you really want to keep clean.

DISTINCTIVE CHARACTERISTICS
Drips gross ghost goo everywhere.

SMELLS LIKE
Melting plastic and old vegetables.

DESCRIPTION
These are some of my least favorite ghosts. They're like regular ghosts but they drip goo everywhere. And they never stop dripping, they never run out of goo. Ghost goo is the worst. Imagine regular goo, but you can't clean it up even though you can touch it and it feels sticky and bad. I don't know if goo ghosts are dripping goo on purpose or if they can't help it but either way I wish they would just stay outside.

DANGEROUS?
They are gross and make me feel gross, and feeling gross can be dangerous if you feel that way all the time.

WHAT TO DO IF YOU SEE ONE
Do whatever you can to get it out of the house. Maybe put a chair outside for it to drip goo on. You could try talking to it about its goo problem but most ghosts don't want to talk about that sort of stuff.

GHOST TYPE
"Poltergeist"

LOCATION
Regular houses.

DISTINCTIVE CHARACTERISTICS
Invisible but very loud and grumpy.

SMELLS LIKE
Burning hats.

DESCRIPTION
Poltergeist ghosts are the only ghosts that you never really see. There are other ghosts that fade in and out but poltergeist are always faded out for some reason. They like to throw stuff and make a general mess of things and I really don't get why they're so upset. Sometimes I'll see an old vase float right in front of my face and just sort of hover for a while before being smashed to the floor. That's a poltergeist being a bozo.

DANGEROUS?
Only to plates and vases and stuff.

WHAT TO DO IF YOU SEE ONE
You won't because they're invisible. If you think you're in a room with a poltergeist you could try turning on the TV or putting on some music. Maybe it's just bored. Being bored can be stressful, even for a spooky ghost.

They are invisible
so I can't show
you what they look
like, I am sorry.
Maybe they look
like this:

GHOST TYPE
"Shadow People"

LOCATION
Wherever a shadow can be.

DISTINCTIVE CHARACTERISTICS
They are people-shaped but made out of shadows.

SMELLS LIKE
Nothing.

DESCRIPTION
Shadow people are when you see the shadow of a huge dude coming up behind you but when you turn around there is no one there. They don't seem to do anything besides spook you out, but I don't trust them because their whole existence is based on tricks. There are a lot of shadow people who hang out where I sleep and it gets really frustrating when I'm just trying to have a relaxing night.

DANGEROUS?
No but you might fall over when you see one and that could be dangerous.

WHAT TO DO IF YOU SEE ONE
Don't give them the satisfaction of seeing you get all spooked out. That's what they're going for and they'll keep doing it to you if they see you getting spooked out even once. You can try to distract them with a shadow puppet show but it never seems to work no matter how hard you practice.

GHOST TYPE
"Grim Reaper"

LOCATION
Wherever someone has died.

DISTINCTIVE CHARACTERISTICS
A big stupid robe and a scythe usually.

SMELLS LIKE
Garbage.

DESCRIPTION
I don't know if there's one grim reaper or a bunch of them but they wig me out and I hope that when I die they don't even bother showing up. Why do they wear those robes? Everyone already knows they're a ghost. And why do they need a scythe? They only mess with people who are dead already, it's unnecessary.

DANGEROUS?
Only if you're dead and really don't want to be.

WHAT TO DO IF YOU SEE ONE
I try to bring them lemonade and apple slices, but they're usually not very hungry. They wig me out but I still try to be friendly. They don't play tricks on me and I appreciate that. Don't try to touch their scythe, they get all weird about it and then you'll feel bad.

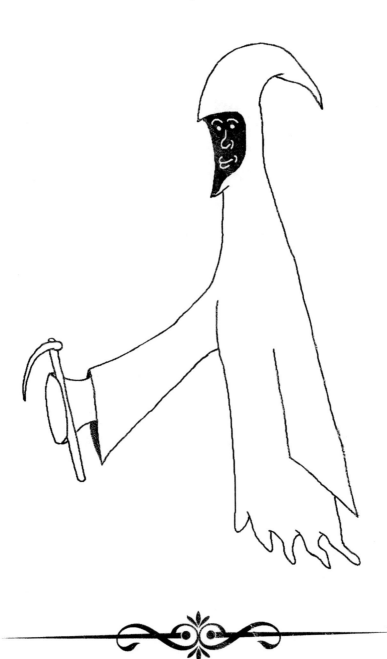

GHOST TYPE
"Gross Reaper"

LOCATION
Anywhere someone has gotten sauce or something on their shirt.

DISTINCTIVE CHARACTERISTICS
They look like grim reapers but they're all dirty and sticky.

SMELLS LIKE
Dirt and bubble gum.

DESCRIPTION
Sometimes I'll spill sauce on my clothes and some sort of reaper will show up and make it even worse. Like I only got sauce on this one tiny part but now a reaper has shown up and made my whole outfit sticky. What is even the point of that? There isn't much else to say about gross reapers outside of how disappointing it is that they exist.

DANGEROUS?
They won't hurt you but they can make a bad day worse.

WHAT TO DO IF YOU SEE ONE
Get ready to take a bath. I put together a gift basket for a gross reaper once. It contained different types of soaps and bubble baths. The reaper took the basket but I never noticed an improvement.

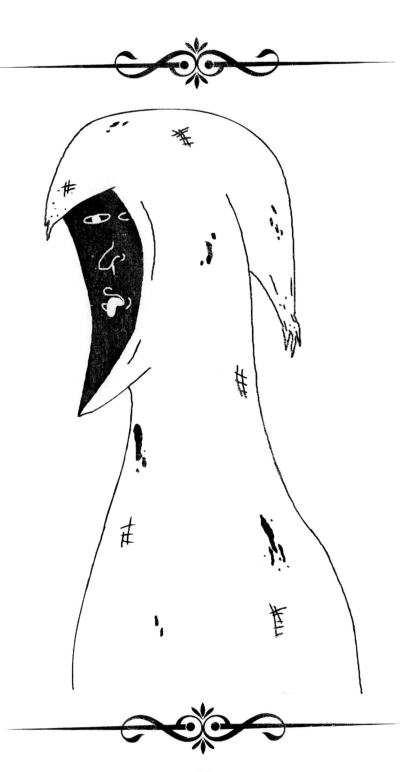

GHOST TYPE
"Ancient King"

LOCATION
Old ruins, majestic fields, dramatic cliffs.

DISTINCTIVE CHARACTERISTICS
Usually wears a crown and carries a scepter.

SMELLS LIKE
Chicken and wine.

DESCRIPTION
Just because you used to be a king doesn't mean I have to do stuff for you. I don't even care. I don't like real kings so I definitely don't like ghost kings. Sometimes I'll see an ancient ghost king and they'll get all grumpy when I don't bow. I'm sorry but how do I even know you're a real king? And even if you are a real king I'm not going to bow to you, I have better things to do.

DANGEROUS?
I guess they could bonk you with their scepter.

WHAT TO DO IF YOU SEE ONE
Just don't even bother trying to argue when them, they won't listen to you even when you know that you're right. They like expensive looking gifts such as pillows and fancy cups, but an ancient king ghost will never give you anything in return.

GHOST TYPE
"Spooky Princess"

LOCATION
Castles, old trees with ribbons on them.

DISTINCTIVE CHARACTERISTICS
Usually dressed like Cinderella or something.

SMELLS LIKE
Cake and bugs.

DESCRIPTION
Spooky princess ghosts usually don't want to talk to me which is fine because I don't want to talk to them. I wish more ghosts would just hang out by old trees and not try to get me to fall over and hurt myself. Every so often one of them will start singing when the moon is out but they can't really sing that well and they only know like three of the words to their ghost songs.

DANGEROUS?
No, except for Jessica who is a murderer.

WHAT TO DO IF YOU SEE ONE
Don't try to sing along with them even if you're really sad because they'll just get this look on their face and fade away. I sometimes put ribbons on trees when they're not around and they seem to appreciate that.

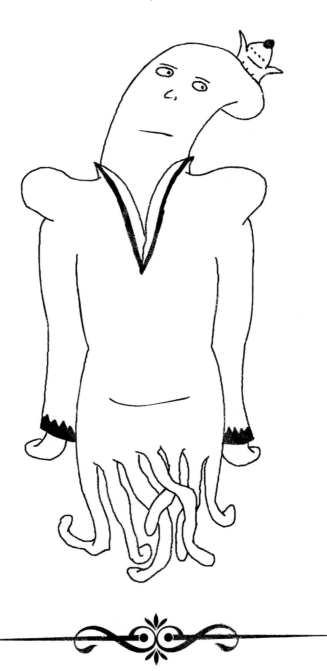

GHOST TYPE
"Ghost Cat"

LOCATION
Old streets, attics, floating right in front of where you're trying to look.

DISTINCTIVE CHARACTERISTICS
Is a cat but a ghost.

SMELLS LIKE
The worst cat food.

DESCRIPTION
Ghost cats are good at seeming like they don't care enough to bother you but they always seem to bother you anyway. Like, I'm trying to read a book, why did you pick this moment to put your ghost cat butt in my face? They don't try to prank you like ghost horses do, but I still don't trust them. There was a ghost cat I named Yogurt who I really liked but then it put its butt in my face and I'm over it.

DANGEROUS?
The ones I've seen don't scratch or bite or anything but you never know with ghost cats.

WHAT TO DO IF YOU SEE ONE
They really like dinner rolls if you want to get one a nice treat. You might feel compelled to pet a ghost cat but your hand will just go right through and then you'll feel even more lonely.

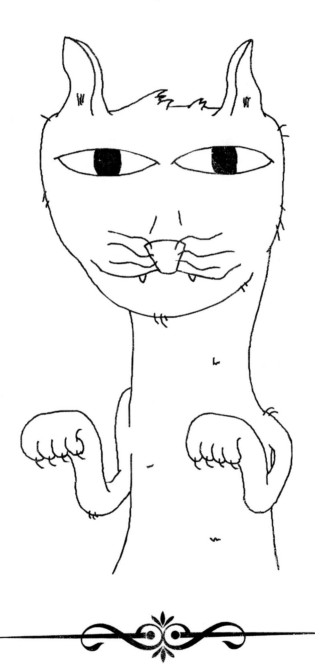

GHOST TYPE
"Prophetic Apparition"

LOCATION
Hanging around old swords or scrolls.

DISTINCTIVE CHARACTERISTICS
Super dramatic.

SMELLS LIKE
Fire and mold.

DESCRIPTION
Prophetic apparitions will pop out of nowhere when you pick up an old sword or a scroll and tell you that you're important, but it's a lie. They'll tell that to anyone. You'll get a good show out of it, with fog and lights and stuff, but they're just trying to get you to run into the woods like a moron.

DANGEROUS?
They might get you to fight a mountain tiger or something stupid like that, and you can't win.

WHAT TO DO IF YOU SEE ONE
Don't listen to them, none of it is true. Come back the next day and they'll tell you something totally different. I wish there was somewhere you could go to file a complaint, because it's pretty much fraud.

GHOST TYPE
"Trapped Ghost"

LOCATION
Basements, sunken ships.

DISTINCTIVE CHARACTERISTICS
Appear to be trapped by some sort of ghost force.

SMELLS LIKE
Soggy snakes.

DESCRIPTION
A trapped ghost is a ghost that appears to be stuck somewhere, like in an invisible box or wedged between two rocks. They'll ask you for help but no matter how hard you try you can't get them free. I wonder if they're really trapped or if they're just trying to waste your time. It's hard to tell with ghosts. They like to trick you but I can also see them getting stuck pretty easily.

DANGEROUS?
No, they'll probably waste your time though.

WHAT TO DO IF YOU SEE ONE
You can try to get them unstuck but it won't work, I'm sorry. There are a lot of trapped ghosts where I live and I make sure to bring them apple slices every day that I can. I've tried to read them stories but I don't think they like that.

GHOST TYPE
"Doug"

LOCATION
Following me.

DISTINCTIVE CHARACTERISTICS
Has the worst face.

SMELLS LIKE
Dry cheese.

DESCRIPTION
I don't know what Doug's deal is, he just follows me around sometimes. Doug is different from other ghosts in that Doug has the worst ghost face. I don't even know if his name is really Doug but he looks like a Doug. He doesn't say anything, he just sort of floats behind me for a while. I wish he would go away forever but I don't think that's going to happen.

DANGEROUS?
No but you might lose your temper.

WHAT TO DO IF YOU SEE ONE
Maybe Doug will talk to you even though he has never talked to me. I don't hate Doug, I just wish I knew why he was such a creep. I hope he figures things out in his weird ghost life.

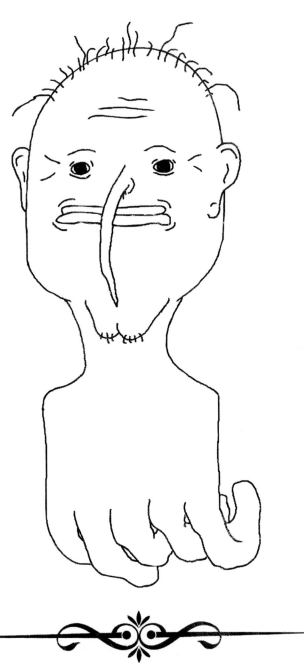

GHOST TYPE
"Baby Ghost"

LOCATION
Small dark rooms, movie theaters, wedged behind sofas.

DISTINCTIVE CHARACTERISTICS
Is a baby and a ghost.

SMELLS LIKE
Peanut butter farts.

DESCRIPTION
Baby ghosts are ghosts that are also babies. They are the stupidest ghosts I've ever met. Imagine a baby, and how stupid it is. Now think about how stupid ghosts are. Ghost babies just sort of float around getting ghost slobber on everything and crying for what feels like weeks. I had ghost babies myself and let me tell you it's no fun when they get hardcore into drugs. Like, what are you even supposed to do about that.

DANGEROUS?
No, they are babies.

WHAT TO DO IF YOU SEE ONE
Just try not to step on it. I don't know if stepping on a ghost baby will hurt it but it feels like something you shouldn't do. They seem to like apple slices, but they also seem to like eating pretty much everything, even dirt. Try to make sure they don't eat anything super gross.

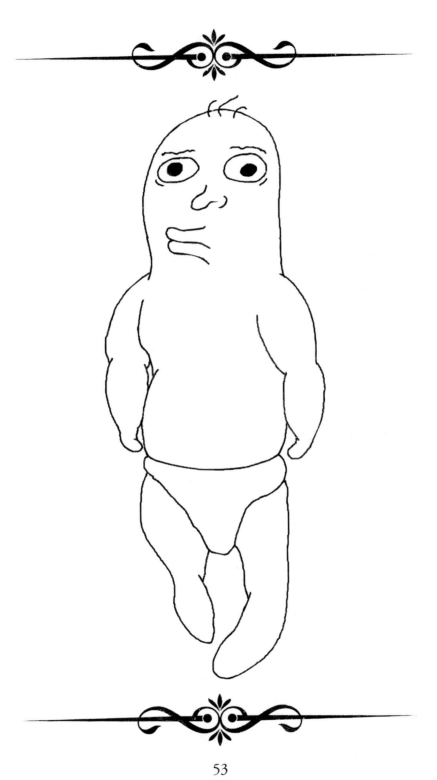

GHOST TYPE
"Angel Ghost"

LOCATION
Old churches, hospitals, Olive Garden.

DISTINCTIVE CHARACTERISTICS
Has wings and a halo and is way too bright, like a flashlight.

SMELLS LIKE
Cookies and sea wind.

DESCRIPTION
I know some people think angels are all special but I think they're just ghosts. They look all majestic and important but when it comes down to it they're just doing all the regular ghost stuff like floating around for no reason. I saw an angel ghost once and thought that maybe we could be friends but it just stuck its tongue out and poked me in the eye.

DANGEROUS?
Yes they will poke you in the eye and it hurts mostly because their pokers are so bright.

WHAT TO DO IF YOU SEE ONE
Angel ghosts make good muses for paintings, at least as far as ghosts go. They don't seem to care about friendship but maybe you can figure out what they do care about and go from there.

GHOST TYPE
"Demon Ghost"

LOCATION
Swamps, carnivals.

DISTINCTIVE CHARACTERISTICS
Horns and weird ghost tails.

SMELLS LIKE
Burning sand.

DESCRIPTION
Everyone thinks demons are scary because they have scare faces but to be honest they don't really bother me. I've never had a demon ghost put its butt in my face or throw a plate at me or anything. They're still ghosts so I'm sure they're up to some sort of tricks but as far as ghosts go I think they're alright. I never see them hanging out with other ghosts so I feel like we probably have a lot in common.

DANGEROUS?
I don't think so but they've got a bunch of pointy parts.

WHAT TO DO IF YOU SEE ONE
They enjoy eating blueberries so it's probably a good idea to keep some in your pockets if you want to get on their good side. If you're thinking about starting a fight with one don't, just leave them alone they aren't hurting anyone.

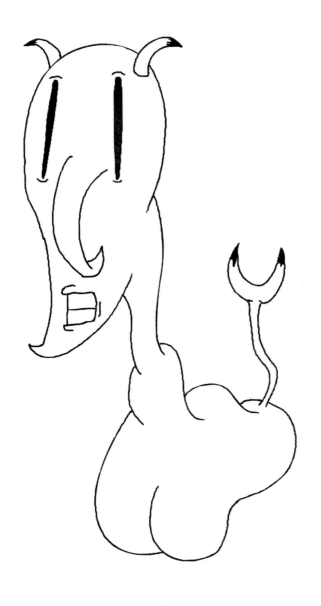

GHOST TYPE
"Doom Spirit"

LOCATION
Bridges, unmaintained buildings, other dangerous places.

DISTINCTIVE CHARACTERISTICS
Stupid skull face.

SMELLS LIKE
Salted fish.

DESCRIPTION
These ghosts tend to show up right before something terrible happens, like a bridge falling over or a large wheel spinning out of control. I don't know if they cause bad things to happen or if they just like to watch. Either way I think these ghosts are no good. I don't like many ghosts but these seem especially bad. It doesn't help that they have skull faces for no reason. It just seems like too obvious a choice for an evil ghost.

DANGEROUS?
Probably, I don't really know.

WHAT TO DO IF YOU SEE ONE
Get to a safe space away from anything that could spiral out of control and smoosh you. Maybe alert the media and local businesses. I hope that things turn out okay for you.

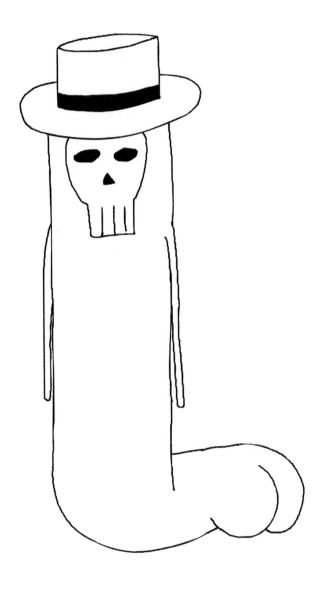

GHOST TYPE
"Ghost Ghost"

LOCATION
Wherever you find ghosts.

DISTINCTIVE CHARACTERISTICS
Is a ghost of a ghost.

SMELLS LIKE
Toast and almond butter.

DESCRIPTION
I don't really know how to explain ghost ghosts. They are ghosts of ghosts. When a ghost dies it becomes a ghost again, but it doesn't become a ghost ghost, so I'm not sure how ghost ghosts came to be. They seem just like regular ghosts, but they're not. They're ghosts of ghosts, but they've never been regular ghosts. It gives me a headache thinking about it. I know that they're ghosts of ghosts but I can't find the words to explain what that means. I am sorry.

DANGEROUS?
I think it's dangerous that they exist but they won't attack you or anything like that.

WHAT TO DO IF YOU SEE ONE
Try and figure out how to explain them and then tell the world. Ghost ghosts don't seem to like apple slices or slices of pretty much anything. Maybe they're just TOO dead.

GHOST TYPE
"Ghost Train"

LOCATION
Abandoned train tracks.

DISTINCTIVE CHARACTERISTICS
Is a train, but also a ghost.

SMELLS LIKE
Coal covered in milk.

DESCRIPTION
The first time I saw a ghost train I thought it was a train for ghosts, but it's not. It's a train that is itself a ghost. I don't know if it's a dead train or a ghost who decided to look like a train, but either way, it's not a good idea to ride one. I can only imagine the stupid place you'd end up if you got on board. You would probably end up in a ghost realm and those are really frustrating. Sometimes a ghost train will have a conductor but that's just a regular ghost who is friends with the ghost train.

DANGEROUS?
I've never gotten on one but probably.

WHAT TO DO IF YOU SEE ONE
Don't get on board, especially if you look in your pocket and see that you have a magical ticket. It's a trick. Still, even though I am suspicious of their intentions I like to wave at them as they drive by.

GHOST TYPE
"Ghost Bus"

LOCATION
Empty city streets at night.

DISTINCTIVE CHARACTERISTICS
Really looks nothing like a bus.

SMELLS LIKE
Feet, beer, and mushrooms.

DESCRIPTION
Ghost trains look a lot like trains, but ghost buses don't really look anything like buses to me. They're trying to fool you into getting inside of them but that's pretty easy to avoid. They have huge stupid ghost faces and so it doesn't look like something you would ever want to climb into. I imagine that if you ever got on a ghost bus it would probably drive you right into a wall. I think ghost buses are some of the stupidest ghosts, and definitely the worst at tricks.

DANGEROUS?
Only if you're stupider than they are.

WHAT TO DO IF YOU SEE ONE
Just find a regular bus if you need to get somewhere. Ghost buses always seem pretty hungry so I try to give them a snack when I can. They enjoy singing and it can be fun to join in, even if you don't know any stupid ghost songs.

BEEP

BEEP

GHOST TYPE
"Lion King"

LOCATION
Wherever you're having a really bad day.

DISTINCTIVE CHARACTERISTICS
Is a big happy lion.

SMELLS LIKE
Trees and apples.

DESCRIPTION
I don't even know if the Lion King is a ghost, but whenever things are really bad he will show up and I'll feel a little better for a while. Ghosts don't usually do nice things like that, but the Lion King disappears into a mysterious fog at the end of the day and that's not a thing that lions do, so I dunno. I wish I could tell the Lion King how much he means to me but I think he already knows, otherwise why would he show up?

DANGEROUS?
No, the Lion King is kind and wonderful.

WHAT TO DO IF YOU SEE ONE
Get ready for one of the best days of your life.

GHOST TYPE
"Bug Ghost"

LOCATION
Back yards, on the ceiling, under furniture.

DISTINCTIVE CHARACTERISTICS
Big and gross and a bug.

SMELLS LIKE
Sweaty grass.

DESCRIPTION
I don't know what would make a ghost decide to look like a big gross bug, but there are a lot of them. They like to crawl all over your body which is very uncomfortable because they are bigger than a person and also they are covered in bug slime. I imagine they find the whole thing super funny, but I do not. There are some ghosts that I can put up with but when I have to hang out with a bug ghost it ruins the rest of my day. What's wrong with dirt, why can't they hang out on the ground outside?

DANGEROUS?
Not that I can tell but they do leave behind way too much slime so be careful you don't slip and slide.

WHAT TO DO IF YOU SEE ONE
Just leave the house for the rest of the day if you can. Be careful to not touch their antenna as that makes them go all bug crazy for a little bit. They don't seem to eat much but they do really like lemonade.

GHOST TYPE
"War Ghost"

LOCATION
Sites of great battles, or even really dumb battles I guess.

DISTINCTIVE CHARACTERISTICS
They usually have a gun or a sword or something.

SMELLS LIKE
Gunpowder and barf.

DESCRIPTION
War ghosts are either ghosts who died in a war or ghosts who died doing something stupid but want to pretend they died in a war. They spend most of their time fighting other ghosts which is fine by me. Every once in a while a war ghost will pop up from behind a sofa and yell at me, but other than that I don't really see them that much. They always have such serious looks on their faces even though their faces are super dumb.

DANGEROUS?
Only really to other ghosts, but when ghosts die they just come back again so whatever.

WHAT TO DO IF YOU SEE ONE
Don't panic, it will probably get in a ghost fight and ghost die and then you'll have the rest of the night free. I've tried to figure out why they're fighting but as far as I can tell it's just because they're ghosts.

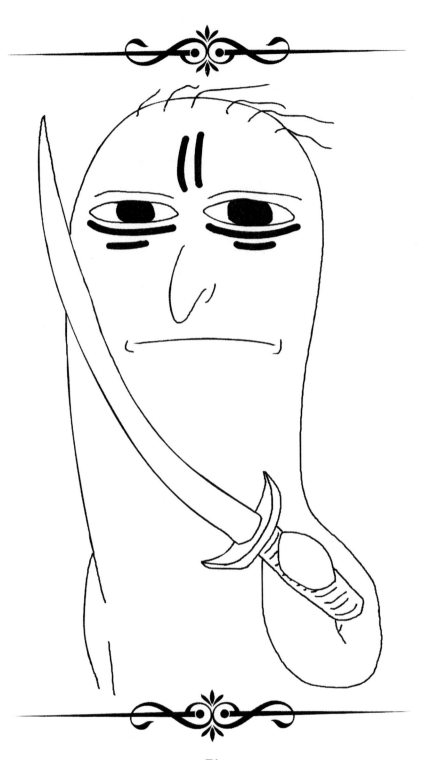

GHOST TYPE
"President Taft Ghost"

LOCATION
Everywhere, but only on September 15th.

DISTINCTIVE CHARACTERISTICS
Looks mostly like US President William Howard Taft.

SMELLS LIKE
Leather and shoe polish.

DESCRIPTION
I don't really understand what the deal is with these ghosts but every September 15th a whole lot of them show up, all looking like President Taft. I think that was Taft's birthday. Maybe President Taft was really important to ghosts. I don't really care enough to think about it. All they do is stand there. Some of them will smoke a pipe, others will spin around a bunch. At the end of the day they vanish and I don't see them again for a year.

DANGEROUS?
No but they make me angry.

WHAT TO DO IF YOU SEE ONE
I guess just plan on not getting a lot done for the rest of the day. There's a lot of them and they don't seem to notice when you need to get important things done.

GHOST TYPE
"Vortex Ghost"

LOCATION
Birthday parties, restaurants, horse racing tracks.

DISTINCTIVE CHARACTERISTICS
Long, twirly bodies.

SMELLS LIKE
Mint, snow and beef gravy.

DESCRIPTION
The only thing that makes a vortex ghost different from a regular ghost is its long, loopy body. Also they tend to hang out in big crowds so that more people can see their loops. I don't really understand what's so special about ghost loops but I suppose it is not for me to know. If you're super into loops then vortex ghosts will probably be your favorite type of ghost. As for me, again I just really don't see what's so special about loops, I'm sorry I just don't.

DANGEROUS?
Not unless you get your head or leg stuck in one.

WHAT TO DO IF YOU SEE ONE
Admire or ignore the loops depending on your preferences. Whatever you do don't try to un-loop the loops. That is the worst thing you can do to a vortex ghost. It doesn't matter how stupid you think loops are, they're important to vortex ghosts and that's all that matters.

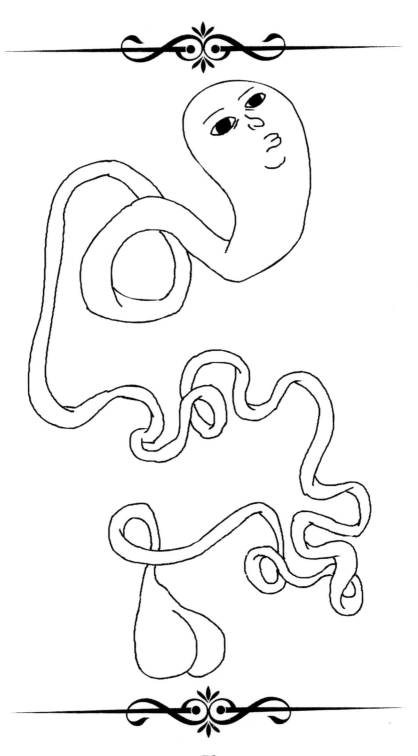

GHOST TYPE
"Dead Ghost"

LOCATION
Most places that regular ghosts are found.

DISTINCTIVE CHARACTERISTICS
They are dead. But like, ghost dead.

SMELLS LIKE
Wet potatoes.

DESCRIPTION
When a ghost dies it comes back as another ghost. But their old dead ghost body doesn't disappear, it just sort of floats around for a while like a gross wet flying sock. It can get really tough to deal with when there's a lot of ghost fighting going on and your house fills up with creepy dead ghost bodies, in addition to the regular ghosts. They eventually go away but I'm not sure where. I worry that other ghosts eat them. I would find that really upsetting and I hope it isn't true.

DANGEROUS?
No but mega gross.

WHAT TO DO IF YOU SEE ONE
Just push it out of the way. You'll get a little ghost goo on your hands but that's bound to happen no matter what.

GHOST TYPE
"Mimic Ghost"

LOCATION
Towns thick with fog, desert islands.

DISTINCTIVE CHARACTERISTICS
They look sort of like you do.

SMELLS LIKE
An electrical fire.

DESCRIPTION
The first time I saw a mimic ghost I thought I had died and I was seeing myself. A mimic ghost will copy your face, but it doesn't really put all that much effort into it. They aren't good enough at mimicry to fool your friends or family or anything but it's a creepy thing to encounter in your day to day life.

DANGEROUS?
They are not aggressive, they are just weirdos.

WHAT TO DO IF YOU SEE ONE
Mimic ghosts will copy almost any face they see, so it can be a fun activity to turn on the TV and have it mimic your favorite celebrity chef or waiter. I once had a mimic ghost copy the face of Emeril Lagasse and that was a special day.

GHOST TYPE
"1950s Watch Salesman Ghost"

LOCATION
Knocking on your front door.

DISTINCTIVE CHARACTERISTICS
Has a ghost briefcase full of ghost watches.

SMELLS LIKE
Old clothes and worms.

DESCRIPTION
Were there that many watch salesmen in the 50s? Because I have seen a lot of these ghosts and I really don't understand why there are so many. And why are they still selling watches when they're dead? Who buys a watch from a ghost, I mean come on. I try to tell them that I don't want a watch but they just stare at me. What's the big idea? I don't need this.

DANGEROUS?
No I don't think so.

WHAT TO DO IF YOU SEE ONE
They are super into coffee and lemonade so it's easy to be hospitable, but don't let yourself get pressured into a sale. The watches they sell are probably stupid ghost watches so they'll go right through your arm.

GHOST TYPE
"Blob Ghost"

LOCATION
Sewers, bathtubs.

DISTINCTIVE CHARACTERISTICS
They are a huge blob.

SMELLS LIKE
Peppermint.

DESCRIPTION
The first time you see a blob ghost you'll probably think "Oh great, now I have to deal with this huge blob of a ghost." But to be honest the blob ghosts are pretty okay. I see them sometimes rolling to and fro, but they don't stick around for long and they don't get any of their blob juice on stuff. I mostly just want ghosts to leave me alone and blob ghosts do. I don't know what happened to turn them into such huge blobs but whatever it was it also turned them into less annoying ghosts.

DANGEROUS?
No, they make an effort to not roll all over you with their huge blob bodies.

WHAT TO DO IF YOU SEE ONE
I don't think they want any attention so try to give them some space. Just sort of say "sup" and then let them blob away.

GHOST TYPE
"Black Knight"

LOCATION
Fields, bridges, castles.

DISTINCTIVE CHARACTERISTICS
They have a knight helmet that they don't need.

SMELLS LIKE
Oil and dirt.

DESCRIPTION
I don't know if this is really its own type of ghost. A black knight ghost will show up and then for the next week all the other ghosts decide they want to be black knights as well. It's a whole week of stupid ghost sword fighting and jumping about. I am so happy when they decide to stop being black knights because it means I can think about stuff again.

DANGEROUS?
Yes, a black knight ghost will just sort of swing its sword everywhere and then all the other ghosts start doing the same thing. What a bunch of bozos.

WHAT TO DO IF YOU SEE ONE
Shoo it away before the other ghosts see. If you end up with a bunch of black knight ghosts you might as well join in on the action, because they pretty much take over the entire ghost house.

GHOST TYPE
"Fairy"

LOCATION
Forests, lakes.

DISTINCTIVE CHARACTERISTICS
Is very small and has wings.

SMELLS LIKE
Cookies and paint.

DESCRIPTION
Years ago when I saw my first fairy I didn't realize that fairies were ghosts. But once you get a good look at their stupid ghost face there is no mistaking it. I assume they have perfect ghost butts as well but they're covered with leaves so I don't know for sure. Sometimes a fairy ghost will follow you home from the woods and then everything in your house gets covered in goo dust. It is a real problem. I wish I didn't have to deal with things like this.

DANGEROUS?
Not really, but they are a big pain.

WHAT TO DO IF YOU SEE ONE
Don't let it follow you home. If you ate in the woods you should check your lunch box, sometimes they hide in there. If a fairy ghost ends up in your house you can get it to leave by running into walls and freaking out a bunch. I think they just get worried that you're going to hurt yourself.

GHOST TYPE
"Chiller"

LOCATION
Mountains, snow covered hills.

DISTINCTIVE CHARACTERISTICS
Super cold and creepy.

SMELLS LIKE
Frozen sloppy joes.

DESCRIPTION
Chillers are some of the meanest ghosts around, but luckily they only show up when it's really cold and snowy. They are always showing their teeth to intimidate you, and it usually works because their teeth are way too big for their face. I don't like looking at them, I need to turn away. They will chase you, but thankfully they aren't super fast. If you get indoors you should be okay, although they will look at you through the window for what seems like forever. I fell asleep once when one was watching me, and when I woke up it was still there but it was drinking a soda or something.

DANGEROUS?
Yes, they are very aggressive and mean.

WHAT TO DO IF YOU SEE ONE
Get inside and make yourself some warm milk because it's going to be a long and spooky night.

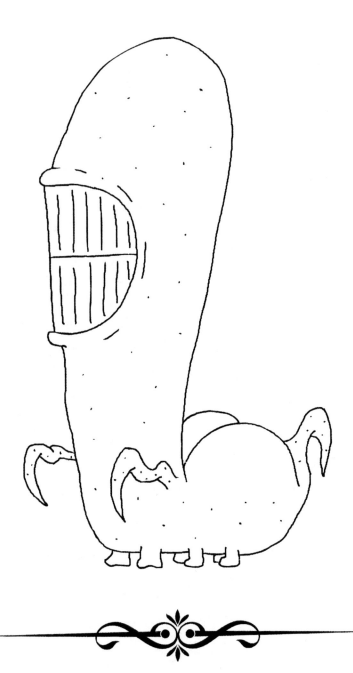

GHOST TYPE
"Crystal Spirit"

LOCATION
Spooky caves.

DISTINCTIVE CHARACTERISTICS
They have huge crystals sticking out of them for no reason.

SMELLS LIKE
Chlorine.

DESCRIPTION
Crystal spirits look like regular ghosts but they have big crystals sticking out of their face. I don't think the crystals serve a purpose but what do I know. If you try to touch one of their crystals they will look at you like "no" and then slowly turn away. The worst thing about crystal spirits is that they always put their perfect ghost butts on your face in pairs. I don't know why but there's always two of them doing it. Their crystals glow when this happens but nothing seems to change beyond that.

DANGEROUS?
Maybe the crystals are radioactive and I'm dying, I don't know.

WHAT TO DO IF YOU SEE ONE
If you see one you should be okay. If you see two you should prepare yourself for a face full of ghost butts. Their crystals are pretty, especially when you have a flashlight to shine at them. I wish I could keep the crystals and leave the ghosts.

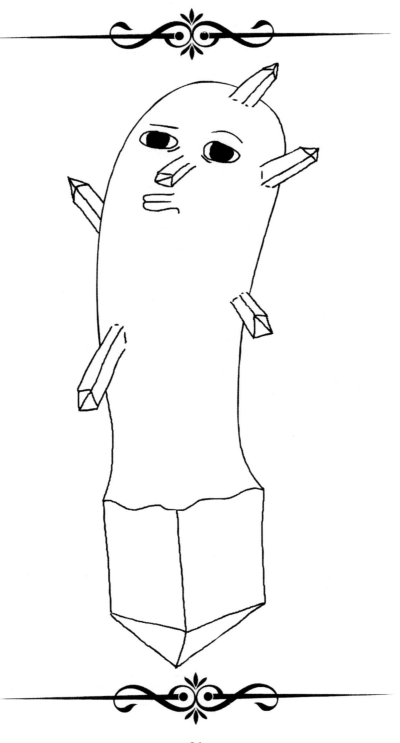

GHOST TYPE
"Vampire Ghost"

LOCATION
Historical landmarks, universities.

DISTINCTIVE CHARACTERISTICS
Vampire teeth and stupid bat wings.

SMELLS LIKE
Old shoes.

DESCRIPTION
Vampire ghosts are ghosts that are pretending to be vampires. I do not believe that they are real vampires, because I know too much about ghost tricks. Still, even though they aren't real vampires it doesn't mean they won't put their gross soggy ghost lips on your neck. It is one of the worst feelings in the world. They don't suck your blood but they definitely suck the hope and joy out of your day. It is unacceptable.

DANGEROUS?
Very dangerous to morale but that's about it.

WHAT TO DO IF YOU SEE ONE
Tell it that you know it's playing a ghost trick and that you don't want it to suck on your neck like some sort of pervert. You have rights and you don't need this in your life.

GHOST TYPE
"Orb"

LOCATION
Everywhere.

DISTINCTIVE CHARACTERISTICS
Is a bright round orb.

SMELLS LIKE
Fried lobster and berries.

DESCRIPTION
These things show up everywhere and I don't know what their deal is. At first glance they look just like a glowing round ball, but when you peek up close you can see their stupid ghost face and sexy ghost butt. I wouldn't mind them so much if there weren't so many of them floating around everywhere I go. It sucks to run into one when you have your mouth open, especially if you get the butt side.

DANGEROUS?
No, I don't think they even do anything.

WHAT TO DO IF YOU SEE ONE
They can be fun to blow around, but be careful that you don't blow too hard or you might fall over. At Christmas you can pretend that they're decorations, as long as you ignore the face and butt parts.

GHOST TYPE
"Forest Spirit"

LOCATION
Anywhere but forests.

DISTINCTIVE CHARACTERISTICS
They have branches and leaves all over them.

SMELLS LIKE
Flowers, old meat, and dog toys.

DESCRIPTION
I have never seen a forest spirit in an actual forest. The only time I see them is when they're trying to tell me how great the forest is and how much better it is than everywhere else. I don't care, I have enough to deal with without worrying about bears and snakes and antlers. They don't even pick up all the leaves they drop, and it can really add up to a whole lot of unnecessary hassle.

DANGEROUS?
No but they won't stop talking about the forest.

WHAT TO DO IF YOU SEE ONE
Do not ask it about the forest, if you do this even once you will never hear the end of it. If you are having a garden related problem they will be glad to help but I don't think they actually know what they're talking about.

GHOST TYPE
"Zoo Keeper Ghost"

LOCATION
Winding roads.

DISTINCTIVE CHARACTERISTICS
Looks a little like a zoo keeper, but only a little.

SMELLS LIKE
All of the animals in the world rolled into a big ball.

DESCRIPTION
I've seen two or three zoo keeper ghosts just sort of floating aimlessly down the street. Maybe when zoo keepers die they don't know what to do because there's not a large variety of animal ghosts. I feel bad for them but I also don't want to talk to them because I'm worried they'll want to talk about zoo keeping. I really don't care about zoo keeping. I've never even been to a zoo. I don't think animals like me even though I like them. So seeing a bunch of animals would just make me feel bad about myself.

DANGEROUS?
No, although I've never approached one.

WHAT TO DO IF YOU SEE ONE
Maybe ask them what's up, if you don't mind possibly talking about zoo keeping. You can offer them some apple slices, although sometimes by the time you get the slices ready the zoo keeper ghost has already faded away. Then you've got a bunch of apple slices and you're not even hungry.

GHOST TYPE
"Super Old Ghost"

LOCATION
Clock towers, grave yards.

DISTINCTIVE CHARACTERISTICS
They are mega old.

SMELLS LIKE
Halloween candy and stale cashews.

DESCRIPTION
I don't know why some ghosts look super old but boy do they look crazy old. It's confusing and weird and I don't like thinking about the implications. Their faces are all wrinkly and I don't get how that is possible. They leave me alone so I leave them alone, but I feel bad because none of the other ghosts seem to talk to them. Maybe they also don't like thinking about the implications. Some super old ghosts wear shoes, even though they don't have ghost feet.

DANGEROUS?
No, they are old and slow.

WHAT TO DO IF YOU SEE ONE
Don't look at it for too long because that would be rude and weird. If you are old maybe you could talk to it about being old or what life was like before the war.

GHOST TYPE
"Ghost of Christmas Past"

LOCATION
Anywhere on Christmas Eve.

DISTINCTIVE CHARACTERISTICS
Looks like a creepy candle.

SMELLS LIKE
Chocolate and plastic.

DESCRIPTION
Every Christmas Eve one of these floats into my bedroom, mumbles something and waves its arms around, and then all of the other ghosts laugh at me. It was a little funny the first time but it's been the same routine every year and I'm sick of it. It's not even that good of a joke. There are so many other famous ghosts they could do but it's always the ghost of Christmas past. Just leave me alone.

DANGEROUS?
They're very warm if you try to hit one.

WHAT TO DO IF YOU SEE ONE
Laugh if you can, because it's going to be the same joke next year and it won't be as funny. You could try dressing up like a different Christmas ghost yourself, but no one ever seems to notice so why put in the effort?

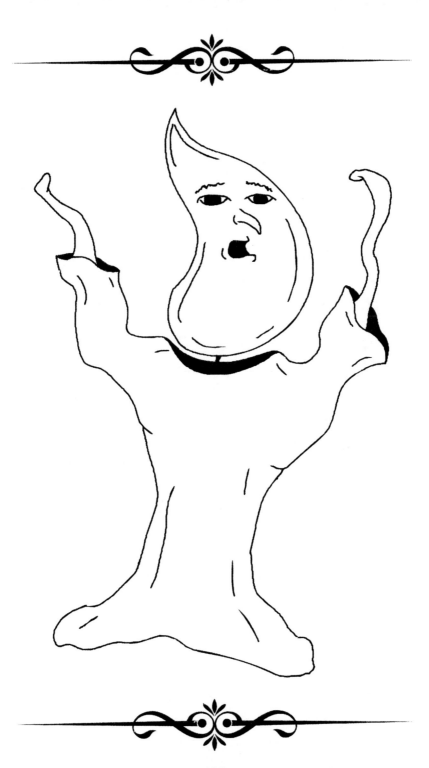

GHOST TYPE
"Toast Ghost"

LOCATION
Kitchens when I'm making food.

DISTINCTIVE CHARACTERISTICS
Is a floating piece of toast with a butt.

SMELLS LIKE
Vinegar.

DESCRIPTION
Are these a trick? I don't know. Ghosts play so many jokes and tricks on me that it can be hard to tell what is real sometimes. I've seen these ghosts in the kitchen and it makes me upset. It's a piece of toast with a butt and no face. Why do they exist? The world of ghosts is diverse but this is going too far. They don't put their toast butts on your face, instead they will just sort of settle down on top of whatever you're trying to eat. Imagine you're just eating a bowl of spaghetti but now it has some toast butt on it. It's times like that when I wonder if it's all worth it.

DANGEROUS?
I stepped on one once and it was slipperier than I would have guessed.

WHAT TO DO IF YOU SEE ONE
Don't try to eat it, it isn't real toast and it's hard to eat around the butt.

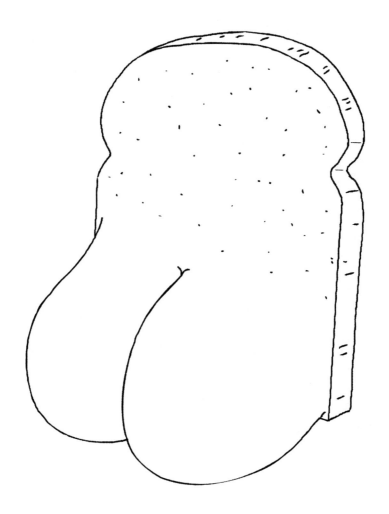

GHOST TYPE
"Ghooooooost"

LOCATION
Everywhere you find regular ghosts.

DISTINCTIVE CHARACTERISTICS
Super long.

SMELLS LIKE
Taco filling and smog.

DESCRIPTION
I call these ghosts "ghooooooosts" because they are much longer than regular ghosts. It's not a very original name but I'm doing my best. They like to trip you using their long ghost bodies and that's a pretty terrible thing to do. The one good thing with ghooooooosts is that you usually don't have to deal with their perfect sexy butts, and that's a rare delight. Overall I don't think these ghosts are that interesting.

DANGEROUS?
They will make you fall over more than almost any other ghost.

WHAT TO DO IF YOU SEE ONE
It's always nice to ask a ghooooooost if it needs help rolling itself up, because their bodies can get pretty unmanageable. The answer is usually no but every once in a while you're able to really help a ghost out and feel like you've done something important.

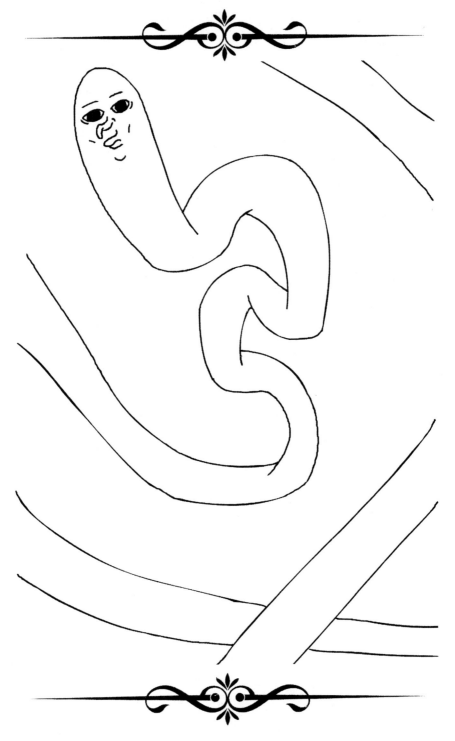

GHOST TYPE
"Ghost Cloud"

LOCATION
The sky.

DISTINCTIVE CHARACTERISTICS
Looks like a cloud but is really a ghost.

SMELLS LIKE
Not sure.

DESCRIPTION
I don't know if they do this as a joke or if that's how they want to live their ghost life, but sometimes I'll look up at the sky and there will be a stupid ghost face or a sexy ghost butt looking back at me. I once saw an airplane fly into a ghost butt and it made me laugh for a second but then I thought about how I would feel if I flew into a ghost butt. I would feel really bad and I would have no one to talk to about it.

DANGEROUS?
It's probably bad for air travel.

WHAT TO DO IF YOU SEE ONE
Ask it if it can turn into a funny shape, like a cow or a triangle. I've never had a ghost cloud listen to me but maybe I've just been too far away.

GHOST TYPE
"Linda from Accounting"

LOCATION
A desk in my closet.

DISTINCTIVE CHARACTERISTICS
Looks kind of like an accountant.

SMELLS LIKE
Fried dough.

DESCRIPTION
Linda is a ghost accountant who lives in my closet, taking up almost all of the room. She is always on the phone and never has time to talk to me. I don't usually want to talk to ghosts but I really want to ask Linda to get out of my closet. I don't have many things but they're all on the floor right now. Why do ghosts even need accountants? I don't think they do. Do ghosts even have money? They probably do, and it probably looks really stupid.

DANGEROUS?
I don't think so but you never know with accountants.

WHAT TO DO IF YOU SEE ONE
If you see Linda that means you're in my room and that's against the law. Don't bother trying to hire her, I've tried to get Linda to do my taxes but she just threw up on my receipts.

GHOST TYPE
"Water Spirit"

LOCATION
Lakes, puddles, sinks.

DISTINCTIVE CHARACTERISTICS
Only hangs out in water.

SMELLS LIKE
Baking soda.

DESCRIPTION
Water spirits are ghosts that have blobbed themselves into a big puddle of water. It's gross when you accidentally sit in one when you're just trying to take a bath. They feel like pudding. They're one of the few ghosts whose butts I haven't seen but I'm sure it's there somewhere. I'm glad I haven't seen it. I wish I had never seen any ghost butts. Maybe just one, to know what I'm dealing with, but then never again.

DANGEROUS?
Probably if you drink one by accident.

WHAT TO DO IF YOU SEE ONE
Don't step in it, no matter how refreshing it looks. I've tried to feed water spirits but they never seem interested. I think they like it when I read to them but it's hard to really tell because they're a motionless ghost liquid.

GHOST TYPE
"Floating Skull"

LOCATION
Dark rooms.

DISTINCTIVE CHARACTERISTICS
Is a big floating skull with stupid noodle arms.

SMELLS LIKE
Rocks and clay.

DESCRIPTION
I think these ghosts are trying to look tough but it isn't working. Why would I be afraid of a skull when I have to deal with spooky ghosts every day of my life? Give me a break. Floating skull ghosts try to scare me by waving their arms around but it just looks stupid. I haven't seen many of these lately so perhaps they got the hint. But ghosts are pretty dumb so I doubt it.

DANGEROUS?
I don't think so.

WHAT TO DO IF YOU SEE ONE
Be careful to avoid its noodle arms, they sort of just wiggle all over the place with no regard for basic decency. I wonder if floating skulls know how ridiculous they are. They probably do.

GHOST TYPE
"Ghost Tree"

LOCATION
Outdoors.

DISTINCTIVE CHARACTERISTICS
A big tree with a ghost face.

SMELLS LIKE
Rain, blueberries and socks.

DESCRIPTION
I can never tell if ghost trees are ghosts living inside trees or ghosts that have become trees or trees that have died and become ghosts. I guess it doesn't really matter in the end, all that matters is that they are ghosts. They don't seem to care much about me so I don't care much about them. They will stare at you if you stare first, but I would do the same thing so I can't judge them for that.

DANGEROUS?
No but they would probably go all ghost crazy if you tried to cut them down or pick their precious ghost fruit.

WHAT TO DO IF YOU SEE ONE
When I see a ghost tree I usually compliment it on its delicious looking ghost fruit. I don't know if that flatters or insults them, because I can't read their stupid tree faces, but it's something to say.

GHOST TYPE
"Ghost Pants"

LOCATION
Stores, supermarkets.

DISTINCTIVE CHARACTERISTICS
They are pants that walk around by themselves.

SMELLS LIKE
Crackers.

DESCRIPTION
Few ghosts make me as angry as ghost pants do. There's nothing worse than having a spooky pair of pants knock over a bunch of shelves at the store and then disappear right when the manager shows up. Why would I knock over a bunch of shelves? No one ever believes me. It's hard enough just leaving the house, and then I have to deal with a bunch of ghost pants pranks when I'm trying to buy some sandwiches.

DANGEROUS?
Yes they can get you in a lot of trouble.

WHAT TO DO IF YOU SEE ONE
Never try to put on a pair of ghost pants. It makes your whole body feel gross and I think the ghost feels the same way.

GHOST TYPE
"2D Rectangle Ghost"

LOCATION
Complete darkness.

DISTINCTIVE CHARACTERISTICS
A big, flat 2D rectangle.

SMELLS LIKE
Nothing.

DESCRIPTION
No ghost gives me the weirds as much as this one. Sometimes when I'm tired of dealing with ghosts I will shut off every light so that I can't see them anymore. But as soon as everything is completely black I can see this 2D rectangle ghost, bright as day. No matter where I am, as soon as it's totally dark I can see it. I don't want to know why or how, I just want it to not be there anymore.

DANGEROUS?
I'm not sure but I don't trust it.

WHAT TO DO IF YOU SEE ONE
Don't ask it any questions. I suspect that it might know pretty much everything and no one should have access to that kind of spooky knowledge. Maybe if you forget what day someone's birthday is you could ask it that.

GHOST TYPE
"Blanket Ghost"

LOCATION
Roaming the streets on Halloween.

DISTINCTIVE CHARACTERISTICS
Looks like a stupid kid with a blanket over them.

SMELLS LIKE
Soap and sea foam.

DESCRIPTION
I guess ghosts think it's super funny to dress up like ghosts for Halloween. I don't think it's funny. I don't dress up like a person, because that would be stupid. I also don't really celebrate Halloween because I have to deal with spooky things every day of my life and it's the worst. I told a blanket ghost that I though it wasn't very funny and it just tickled my stomach and put ghost goo in my left ear. What a jerk.

DANGEROUS?
Yes, they will put ghost goo in your ear if you just try to tell them your opinions.

WHAT TO DO IF YOU SEE ONE
Don't give them any candy, ghosts don't eat candy so it'll just go to waste. They like it when you pull their blanket off because they always have another blanket underneath.

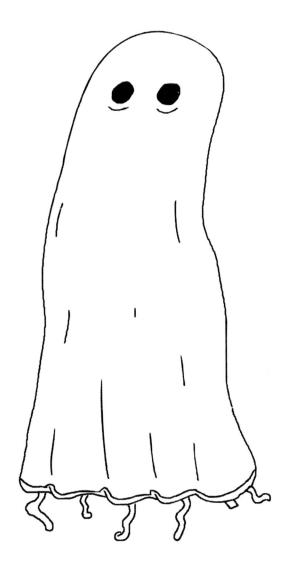

GHOST TYPE
"Santa Claus"

LOCATION
Up in the sky somewhere.

DISTINCTIVE CHARACTERISTICS
Looks pretty much like Santa Claus.

SMELLS LIKE
Not sure.

DESCRIPTION
I don't know if Santa died or if he was always a ghost, but I sometimes see a ghost that looks a lot like him floating over the house. I yelled his name once but he didn't look. It might just be a ghost who died in a Santa costume, who knows. I hope that if Santa did die he finds forgiveness for not caring at all about starving African children.

DANGEROUS?
Probably not, it's Santa.

WHAT TO DO IF YOU SEE ONE
Try to find out if he's the real Santa, because if he is then the world needs to know. And if you ever see a reindeer ghost or an elf ghost, tell them about Santa Claus ghost. They should probably be with him, unless they had a terrible falling out because Santa's a racist.

GHOST TYPE
"Old Book"

LOCATION
Spooky old libraries, secret alchemy rooms.

DISTINCTIVE CHARACTERISTICS
Looks like an old book, except for the ghost face and butt.

SMELLS LIKE
Hamburger wrappers.

DESCRIPTION
I don't think these old ghost books have anything written on them, I think they just want people to open them so they can shoot out wind and lighting and stuff like some sort of dork. They wait for super long periods of time on shelves or on pedestals just waiting to be opened so they can go all ghost crazy. I don't think the joke is all that funny but at least they put a lot of time into it, which is more than I can say about most ghost tricks.

DANGEROUS?
You could probably fall over if you opened one.

WHAT TO DO IF YOU SEE ONE
If you need to blow away a bunch of leaves or dust or something an old ghost book can be pretty useful. Just be careful about the butt part because it can be hard not to touch it.

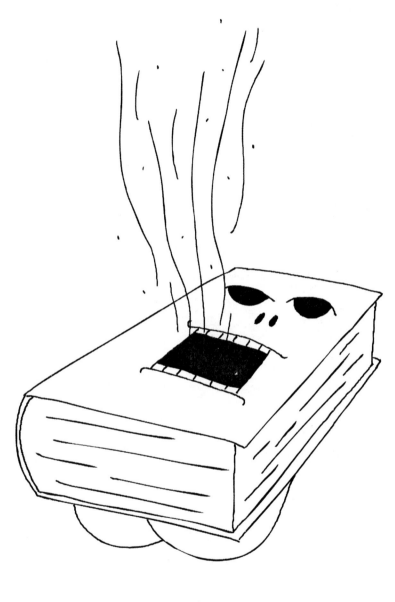

GHOST TYPE
"Enchanted Lake Ghost"

LOCATION
Enchanted lakes.

DISTINCTIVE CHARACTERISTICS
Alluring and mysterious.

SMELLS LIKE
Grocery store sushi.

DESCRIPTION
These ghosts try to lure people into lakes by looking all ghost sexy but I don't think it ever works. I think it's pretty obvious what they're trying to do. Even a bozo would probably not fall for it. I tried to get one of them to come out of the water but it just threw a rock at me. The rock missed but those events confirmed my suspicions and hurt my feelings. I find it hard to make friends and when I really put the effort in I usually get stuff thrown at me, which makes me want to try even less.

DANGEROUS?
Yes, they throw rocks and will probably try to drown you if given the chance.

WHAT TO DO IF YOU SEE ONE
Just leave them alone, they're up to no good and wouldn't make very good friends anyway. If you follow them into a lake and everything turns out fine let me know, because I really want to go into that lake.

GHOST TYPE
"Me?"

LOCATION
The ghost house.

DISTINCTIVE CHARACTERISTICS
Looks like me because it is me.

SMELLS LIKE
Probably the old blankets I sleep on.

DESCRIPTION
I don't know if I'm a ghost but I have my suspicions. I'm including myself in this catalogue of ghosts just in case it turns out that I am one of them. I hope that I'm not but you can never be too sure about anything when it comes to ghosts. I don't remember much about my life and that's a pretty big sign that I might be a ghost. But I can't float through things and I fall down a lot which makes me think I might not be a ghost. If it turns out I'm not a ghost you can just tear this page out of the book.

DANGEROUS?
I don't think so but I do get angry sometimes.

WHAT TO DO IF YOU SEE ONE
I know I can be unpleasant but it would be really nice to talk to someone who isn't a ghost.

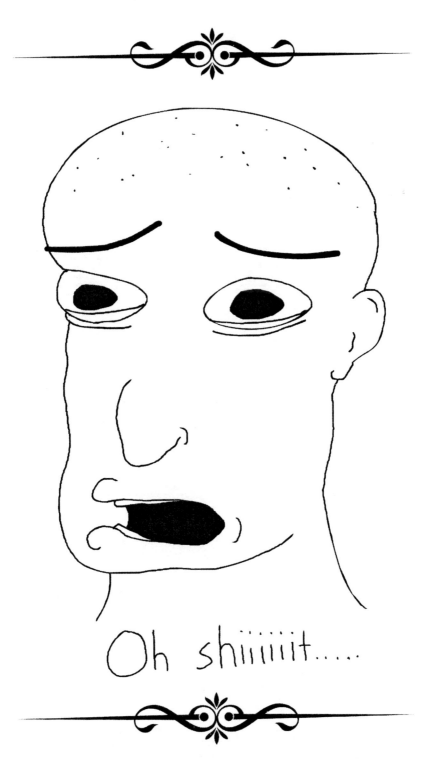

Final Words

Now that you have read this book I hope that you feel better prepared to deal with ghosts in your day to day routine, such as taking showers and going to the store for bread. There is nothing worse than encountering some sort of spooky ghost when you're just trying to brush your teeth or something.

I wish I had a book like this when I first started seeing ghosts. But I didn't, and for a while things were really hard for me. Things are still pretty hard but I am used to it. I am used to the ghosts and their tricks.

In a thousand years perhaps the ghosts will be gone, but for now we have to deal with them. For now we have to let them put their butts on our faces because there isn't much we can do about it. I really wish there was but there isn't.

Life is strange sometimes. I feel angry a lot but not always for a reason. The ghosts do not help with this. I wish ghosts would leave me alone. Sometimes it's nice having them around because I don't have anyone else but mostly it's just the worst.

If you are a ghost and you got through this whole book then well played, I underestimated your interest in books. Please stop playing tricks on me, it's not as funny as you think. Sometimes it's clever but let's be honest 90% of the time it's just you being a stupid ghost. If you're not a ghost then this paragraph was not meant for you.

Don't forget to eat today if you can, if not you might fall over. Three meals a day is the sweet spot but sometimes that just isn't going to happen.

I hope you have a great day, please read me again sometime. One day things will be okay.

Thanks